An [illegible]

Tattva Jnana

Knowledge of the Principles

A curriculum for study by the Priests and Priestesses of Devi Mandir

Prepared by
Swami Satyananda Saraswati
Shree Maa

This study guide is dedicated to Shree Maa, who continually inspires the best within us.

Tattva Jñāna, First edition

ISBN 1-877795-62-3
Library of Congress Catalog

Tattva Jñāna, Swami Satyananda Saraswati
1. Hindu Religion. 2. Goddess Worship. 3. Spirituality.
4. Philosophy. I. Saraswati, Swami Satyananda.

Published by
Devi Mandir Publications
5950 Highway 128
Napa, CA 94558 USA
707-966-2802
www.shreemaa.org

Tattva Jñāna

Knowledge of the Principles
Tat means That
Tva means You
Tattvas are the principles that are you
These principles are the road maps to the understanding of who we are

Kāmakalā

Kāmakalā means the Desired Attribute
Kāmakalā means the Attribute of Desire
Kāmakalā means the harmony of all the threes

The Three Guṇas

Qualities of Nature

Sattva	Rajas	Tamas
truth, light	colors	darkness
pure being	becoming	rest
activity	desire	knowledge

The Threes are Everywhere

Gross Body

Pratyakṣa

What can be perceived through the senses

Subtle Body

Pratyaya

What can be conceived in the mind

Causal Body

Prakāśa

What can be known through meditation or intuition

A U M

And Pervade Everything

Brahmā	Viṣṇu	Śiva
Mahāsarasvatī	Mahālakṣmī	Mahākālī
Creation	Preservation	Transformation

There is no where they are not

Beginning	Middle	End
Past	Present	Future
Aiṃ	Hrīṃ	Klīṃ

There are five constituent elements of existence

Earth	Kṣiti
Water	Apa
Fire	Teja
Air	Maruta
Ether	Baum

These are Perceived on Seven Levels of Consciousness

1. **bhūḥ**
   the gross body
2. **bhuvaḥ**
   the subtle body
3. **svaḥ**
   the causal body
4. **mahaḥ**
   the great body of existence
5. **janaḥ**
   the body of knowledge
6. **tapaḥ**
   the body of light
7. **satyaṃ**
   the body of truth, consciousness, bliss

The Seven Levels of Consciousness

1. the gross body
   perceivable through the senses
2. the subtle body
   conceivable in the mind
3. the causal body
   known through intuition
4. the great body of existence
   all that is knowable
5. the body of knowledge
   all knowledge
6. the body of light
   all light into which the
   knowledge dissolves
7. the causal body
   the intuitive world of infinite
   consciousness, true being, and
   the ultimate bliss

All life manifests to achieve four objectives

1. **Dharma**
to manifest an ideal of Perfection

2. **Artha**
to acquire those physical resources necessary to maintaining that ideal

3. **Kāma**
the cessation or the fulfillment of every other desire except the desire for unity

4. **Mokṣa**
liberation, otherwise known as self-realization

All humans are born owing three debts of karma

1. **Devaṛṇ**
owed to the gods

2. **Pitriṛṇ**
owed to the ancestors

3. **Ācāryaṛṇ**
owed to our gurus and teachers

The debt that we owe to the gods is discharged by making a contribution to this world.

We must make the world a better place because of our having been here.

The debt that we owe to the ancestors is discharged by demonstrating respect through our actions in this world.

We must respect the elderly the way we will want to be respected when we are old and we must teach the next generation the way we want this world to become.

The debt that we owe to our gurus and teachers is discharged by living in accordance with the wisdom that they have taught.

Liberation means being free from debt.

To become free from debt human life has been divided into four parts

1. **Brahmācārya**
2. **Gṛhastha**
3. **Vanaprastha**
4. **Sannyāsa**

Brahmācārya means someone who moves with God. It generally indicates student life, where we learn how shall we make our contribution to the world.

Gṛhastha means who lives in a house, who lives under a roof - generally a married life, where we make our contribution to this creation. We make this world a better place because of our having been here.

Vanaprastha means who lives in the forest - one foot in the house, one foot out of the house, where we consult and manage from afar.

Sannyāsa means who has established truth within, who is totally independent, and lives only in the truth and love of God.

Śāṅkarācarya divided the Sannyāsins into ten tribes called Dasnāmi

1. Bhārati	full of light
2. Giri	live in the mountains
3. Puri	live in cities
4. Saraswati	scholars
5. Van	live in forests
6. Araṅya	live in groves
7. Tirtha	live in pilgrimage places
8. Pārvat	live in the high mountains
9. Sāgar	live at the ocean
10. Nāth	defenders of the faith

There are four aspects of every activity

Dhyāna means meditation or attentiveness.
Jñāna is knowledge or wisdom.
Bhakti means devotion.
Karma means activity.

In every activity some knowledge must exist, and some degree of attentiveness is required in order to bring that activity to fruition.

To the extent one is devoted, to that extent we pay attention.

So every activity requires that knowledge, attention, and devotion be present, and thus they are not severable.

All four exist in every activity.

There are ten Saṃskāras, rites of passage, for every householder to perform

1. **Garbādhāna**
Placing the seed

2. **Sīmantonnayana**
Blessing the fetus and the mother

3. **Jātakarma**
Birth ceremony

4. **Annaprāśana**
First solid food

5. **Vidyārambha**
Learning the alphabets

6. **Upanayana**
Initiation with Gāyatrī mantra and investiture of the sacred thread

7. **Vedāramba**
Commencement of education

8. **Samāvartana**
Graduation from studies

9. **Vivāha**
Marriage

10. **Antyeṣṭī**
Funeral rites

Every organism requires four types of functions

Intelligence system
Immune or defence system
Circulatory system
System for providing nutrition and taking away refuse

In society these are known as:

Brahmaṇas are the intelligence system

Kṣatriyas are the immune or defence system

Vaiśyas are the circulatory system

Kṣūdras are responsible for providing nutrition and taking away refuse.

There are five kośas, sheaths or coverings

1. **annamaya**
   of the consistency of matter
2. **prāṇamaya**
   of the consistency of air
3. **manamaya**
   of the consistency of thought
4. **vijñānamaya**
   of the consistency of light
5. **ānandamaya**
   of the consistency of sat chit ānanda,

true existence
infinite consciousness,
pure bliss

There are eight kinds of behavior for spiritual seekers

1. Vaisṇavācaraṇa

2. Vedikācaraṇa

3. Śivācaraṇa

4. Vāmācaraṇa

5. Dakṣiṇācaraṇa

6. Siddhāntācaraṇa

7. Yogācaraṇa

8. Kulācaraṇa

Vaisṇavācaraṇa

means the behavior of inspiration

Vedikācaraṇa

means the behavior of knowledge

Śivācaraṇa

means the behavior of practice

Vāmācaraṇa

means the beloved behavior, adapting the practice into our lives.

Dakṣiṇācaraṇa

means the preferred behavior, reducing our necessity to act in the world.

Siddhāntācaraṇa

means behavior according to the scriptures.

There are seven parts to behavior in accordance with the scriptures

1. Pūjā
2. Pāṭh
3. Homa
4. Sangīta
5. Nṛta
6. Pravacana
7. Ārpanaṃ

Pūjā means worship.

Pāṭh means recitation of scriptures

Homa means sacred fire ceremonies

Sangīta means singing about God

Nṛta means dancing for God

Pravacana means the explanation of what we are doing and why we are doing it.

Ārpanaṃ means the offering of service.

Yogācaraṇa
means the behavior of union

Kulācaraṇa
means the behavior of excellence

Sitting in one-pointed
samādhi or interacting
with the world is performed
with the same bhāva.

The study of Saṃskṛt has six subjects

1. **Vyākaraṇa** is the study of grammar

2. **Uccāraṇa** is the study of pronunciation

3. **Itihāsa** and **sāhitya** is the study of history and literature

4. **Darśana śastra** is the study of philosophy

5. **Jyotiṣa** is the study of astrology

6. **Paddhoti** is the study of the synthesis through which offering is made

There are seven meters of classical Saṃskṛt

1. **Gāyatrī** contains 24 syllables in each verse
2. **Uṣṇik** contains 28 syllables in each verse
3. **Anuṣṭup** contains 32 syllables in each verse
4. **Bṛhatī** contains 36 syllables in each verse
5. **Paṅktiḥ** contains 40 syllables in each verse
6. **Tṛṣṭup** contains 44 syllables in each verse
7. **Jagatī** contains 48 syllables in each verse

The Path of Sound

Śabda brahmān is the sound of God, the infinite sound of the universe.

Bindu is the first point of sound made manifest.

Nāda is the subtle vibration of sound.

Bījā is the closest audible expression of what the subtle vibration is saying.

Śabda is an audible sound.

Mantra is a sound which takes away the mind.

Vedic śabda are the sounds which describe the wisdom of union.

Bautika śabda are the sounds which describe the world outside

Controlling worldly descriptions, dissolve all sounds into the wisdom of union. Letting go of all thoughts, contemplate the audible expression of the subtle vibration. Becoming more and more subtle, enter into the bindu, where the first point of sound is made manifest. From the bindu, merge into the sound of God, the infinite sound of the universe.

Cārvāka Philosophy

Cārvāka believes in the doctrine of Lokāyata, that only the existence of this material world can be proved. It declares that everything that is in the mind was once in the senses. All we can know, all we can think about, comes through our senses. Pratyakṣa means knowledge derived through the senses.

There are six classical schools of philosophy

1. Nyāya

2. Vaiśeṣika

3. Śāṅkhyā

4. Yoga

5. Pūrva mīmāṃsā

6. Uttara mīmāṃsā

Nyāya

Nyāya says we have forms of knowledge in addition to those of the senses:

Pratyakṣa means knowledge derived through the senses.

Anumāna means inference both deductive and inductive.

Upamāna means comparison or analogy by finding essential similarities.

Śabda means verbal knowledge or testimony.

Prakāśa means what can be known through meditation or intuition.

Vaiśeṣika

1. Substance
2. Quality
3. Activity
4. Generality
5. Particularity
6. Inherence

There are nine constituent elements which comprise the perception of all things:

1. Earth
2. Water
3. Fire
4. Air
5. Ether
6. Time
7. Space
8. Mind
9. Soul

Truly, existence is composed
of eternal invisible atoms uniting
in the vortex of empty space.

Śāṅkhyā

Śāṅkhyā proclaims that atoms alone are not sufficient to explain this existence. In addition to Prakṛti, the embodiment of Nature, we require Puruṣa, the individual soul or consciousness.

Śāṅkhyā proclaims twenty-four principles by which Prakṛti is expressed:

1. Ahaṃkāra
2. Citta
3. Buddhi
4. Man

5. Sight
6. Sound
7. Smell
8. Taste
9. Feel

10. Earth
11. Water
12. Fire
13. Air
14. Ether

15. Eyes
16. Ears
17. Nose
18. Tongue
19. Skin

20. Upper appendages
21. Lower appendages
22. Tongue
23. Reproductive Organs
24. Anus

These twenty-four are witnessed by Consciousness known as Puruṣa.

Yoga

Yoga defines the purpose of life as the perfection of union between the Puruṣa and Prakṛti, and establishes eight steps in the process of that attainment.

There are eight steps
in the path of Yoga:

1. Yama

2. Niyama

3. Āsana

4. Prāṇāyāma

5. Pratyāhāra

6. Dhāraṇā

7. Dhyāna

8. Samādhi

Yama means to take control. Define the goal and define the path.

Niyama means make a discipline. Budget our time, budget our energy, budget our resources.

Āsana means to make the body sit still. Every movement of the body is a reflection of the movement of the mind.

There are four postures conducive for Meditation:

Padmāsana is the full lotus.
Swastikāsana or **Siddhāsana** means interlocking your feet with the heel in the anus.
Vīrāsana is sitting on your hamstrings or sitting back on your heels.
Badrāsana is the diamond pose.

Prāṇāyāma means control of the breath.

There are five kinds of breath:
Prāṇa is inhalation.
Āpāna is exhalation.
Udāna is bringing the breath up.
Samāna is holding it absolutely still and equalized.
Vyāna is an involuntary expulsion.

There are three phases to each breath:
Pūraka is inhalation.
Kumbhaka is retention.
Recaka is expulsion.

The classical Prāṇāyāma
ratio is 1:4:2.

Pratyāhāra means to bring the senses inside to a point of focus.

Dhāraṇā means contemplation.
In contemplation there are three:
a subject
an object
and a relationship

Dhyāna means meditation.
In meditation there are only two:
a subject
an object
The relationship is so intense
that it is intuitively understood.
There is no name by which to call it.

Samādhi means the perfection of union.

There is only one.

There are three types of samādhi

1. Bhāva samādhi
2. Savikalpa samādhi
3. Nirvikalpa samādhi

Bhāva samādhi is an attitude of awareness or communion.

Savikalpa samādhi is communion with an idea. Separation exists.

Nirvikalpa samādhi is communion without any idea.

There are five aspects of samādhi

1. Sālokya
2. Sāmipya
3. Sarūpā
4. Sadṛṣya
5. Sayūja

Sālokya

Sālokya means in the paradigm of reality, in the same loka, in the same world together.

Sāmipya

Sāmipya means with the same activity. Just as the deity is performing, so also I am performing.

Sarūpā

Sarūpā means with form. Just as is Her form, so also is my form. I am looking in a mirror.

Sadṛṣya

Sadṛṣya means with perception. Just as She is perceiving me, so also I am perceiving Her. We have the same perception, and there are only the two of us in existence. There is no third alternative.

Sayūja

Sayūja means with union, or the perfection of union.

Pūrva mīmāṃsā

Pūrva mīmāṃsā actually means Tantra, the synthesis of all spiritual knowledge offered with devotion.

Tantra means to weave, like the warp and the woof of a cloth, weaving together the various forms of knowledge into one discipline.

There are thirty-six principles of Tantra

1. Sadāśiva is pure consciousness
2. Śakti is unlimited energy
3. Iśvara is the principle of union between Śiva and Śakti.

Also called Ardanārīśvara, both male and female.

4. Śuddha Vidyā is pure knowledge.

You have seen the picture of Śiva with his eyes just barely starting to open, when Śiva says, I have a feeling that there is something else out there other than me.

5. Māyā means that She is different from me. I am Śiva and there She is, the Divine Mother, the measurement or limitation of consciousness.

Kāñchūkas

Māyā is perceived through five kāñchūkas, limitations, or modes of perception.

6. Kāla - time
7. Nyāti - space
8. Rāga - activity, being or becoming
9. Vidyā - knowledge of name and form
10. Kalā - attributes

First Ten Principles in Descending Order

1. Sadāśiva
2. Śakti
3. Iśvara
4. Śuddha Vidyā
5. Māyā
6. Kāla
7. Nyāti
8. Rāga
9. Vidyā
10. Kalā

11. Puruṣa is the individual soul or consciousness
12. Prakṛti is the embodiment of Nature.

Antaḥkaraṇa

The next four principles together are called the antaḥkaraṇa, the inner cause or inner sense.

13. Ahaṃkāra
14. Citta
15. Buddhi
16. Man

Ahaṃkāra is the ego, the sense of I.

Citta is the totality of all cognition comprised of buddhi and man.

Buddhi means objective knowledge, or what is, all of the nouns and verbs of experience.

Man is subjective knowledge, or what we think about things. Man comprises the adjectives and adverbs.

Buddhi and Man

Buddhi says this is a book.

Man says this is a good book.

The good is the interpretation of man. Both together are citta, objective and subjective experience, the world as it is and the world as we think it to be, our relationship to it.

The next 20 principles define the gross world and our relationship to it.

Tanmātras

The five Tanmātras are the objects of perception:

1. Sight
2. Sound
3. Smell
4. Taste
5. Feel

Mahābhūtas

The five Mahābhūtas are the essential elements of existence:

1. Earth
2. Water
3. Fire
4. Air
5. Ether

Jñānendriyas

The five Jñānendriyas are the organs of knowledge:

1. Eyes
2. Ears
3. Nose
4. Tongue
5. Skin

Karmendriyas

The five karmendriyas are the organs of action:

1. the upper appendages
2. lower appendages
3. the tongue
4. reproductive organs
5. anus

These principles disclose how divinity descended into manifested existence. In order to go back to that origin, we must return by the same path.

Reverse the Process

Begin by controlling the organs of action, because they are the ones that interact with the outside world.

Control the karmendriyas, the organs of action, and then the jñānendriyas, the organs of knowledge.

Recognize the five elements of existence and their five objects of perception in the subtle body: earth, water, fire, air, ether; sight, sound, smell, taste, and feeling. Let your energy climb the cakras, and put the twenty principles into the balance of harmony.

Now put man, buddhi, citta, into balance. Control the ego, ahaṃkāra.

This is the body of Prakṛti, the body of Nature expressed through the individual, perceived by Puruṣa.

This Puruṣa has been perceived in time, space, activity, knowledge, and with attributes.

By moving beyond these modes of perception, which constitute thirty-one principles, we move into māyā. Then we see Śiva in śuddha vidyā, faintly aware that there is an other, duality, outside. Let him close his eyes.

Iśvara is next, then Śakti and Sadāśiva. These are the thirty-six principles, which are the path to absorption in the unmanifest.

Thirty-six Principles in Descending Order

1. Sadāśiva
2. Śakti
3. Iśvara
4. Śuddha Vidyā
5. Māyā
6. Kāla
7. Nyāti
8. Rāga
9. Vidyā
10. Kalā
11. Puruṣa
12. Prakṛti
13. Ahaṃkāra
14. Citta
15. Buddhi
16. Man
17. Sight
18. Sound
19. Smell
20. Taste
21. Feel

22. Earth
23. Water
24. Fire
25. Air
26. Ether
27. Eyes
28. Ears
29. Nose
30. Tongue
31. Skin
32. Upper appendages
33. Lower appendages
34. Tongue
35. Reproductive Organs
36. Anus

Pūjā paddhoti is the method through which the journey is made.

In worship we synthesize our knowledge of the subjects of Saṃskṛt with the understanding of Philosophy, the practices of Yoga, and by adding the quality of devotion which focuses our attention, we move awareness through the cakras to unite energy with consciousness.

There are seven centers of energy in a human body

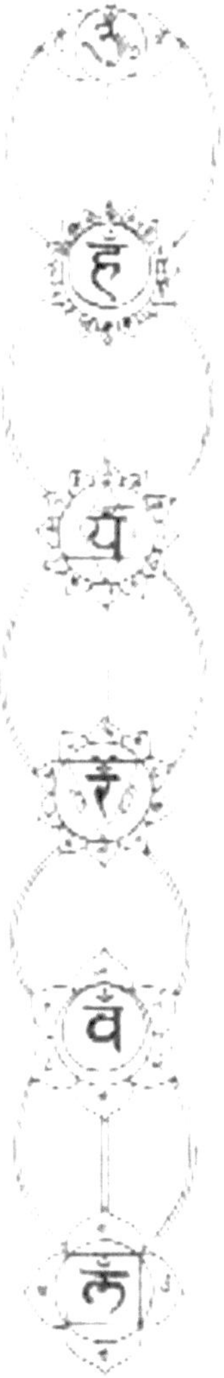

The Seven Cakras

Mulādhāra	(1st Cakra)	Earth	Indra	Laṃ	लं
Swādiṣṭhana	(2nd Cakra)	Water	Varuṇa	Vaṃ	वं
Maṇipura	(3rd Cakra)	Fire	Agni	Raṃ	रं
Anahata	(4th Cakra)	Air	Vāyu	Yaṃ	यं
Viśuddha	(5th Cakra)	Ether	Soma	Haṃ	हं
Āgnyā	(6th Cakra)	Ultimate	Īśvara	Oṃ	ॐ

The Seventh cakra is the Sahasrara, the lotus of a thousand petals at the crown of the head, Mount Kailaśa, where Lord Śiva always dwells, from which the soul exits at the time of leaving the body.

In the Rāmāyaṇa nine steps of Devotion are explained:

1. Associate with saintly people
2. Enjoy stories of divinity and divinely inspired beings
3. Feel the privilege to perform selfless service as an expression of love
4. Sing about divinity without any selfish motivation
5. Recite mantras with full faith
6. Perform all actions with tranquility, and see every circumstance as an opportunity to manifest perfection
7. See the world as equal to God, and regard the company of saintly beings as a greater opportunity than the perception of God
8. Be satisfied with whatever we receive as the fruit of our actions, and do not contemplate the faults of others
9. Remain with simplicity all the time, renounce conniving for selfish ends, and take delight in faith in God with neither exultation nor unhappiness

There are four Vedas

Ṛg Veda
Yajur Veda
Sāma Veda
Atharva Veda

From each Veda has come forth one Mahāvākya, one great statement:

From the Ṛg Veda
Prajñānaṃ Brahmā
The Wisdom of Nature is God

From the Yajur Veda
Tattvamasi
That is You

From the Atharva Veda
Ayamātma Brahmā
This Soul is God

From the Sāma Veda
Ahaṃ Brahmāsmi
I am the Supreme Divinity

The four Vedas were divided each into four parts:

Saṃhitās are the hymns

Brahmāṇas describe the systems of worship

Araṇyākas are the tales of the ṛṣis living in the forests, the stories of the gods and the kings, and the applications of spiritual knowledge

Upaniṣādas are the philosophy

There are Upavedas as well, which discuss other branches of knowledge, for example:

Āyurvedaḥ - The Knowledge of Life
Dhanurvedaḥ - The Knowledge of Weapons
Sthāpatyavedaḥ - The Knowledge of Constructing things that Remain

There are five principle deities to whom devotion can be offered according to the traditions of worship:

Śiva
Viṣṇu
Śakti, The Divine Mother
Gaṇeśa
Sūrya and the Nine Planets

Worship can be as simple or as complex as anyone chooses

Worship can be performed with any of four articles

Whoever offers Me even a leaf, a flower, a fruit, or some water with devotion, I accept that offering of devotion from the soul who makes effort.

Bhagavad Gītā 9:26

Worship can be performed with five articles

1. Lights
2. Incense
3. Flowers
4. Food offering
5. Water

Worship can be performed with ten articles

1. Lights
2. Incense
3. Flowers
4. Food offering
5. Water
6. Cloth
7. Umbrella
8. Fly whisk
9. Fan
10. Mirror

Worship can be performed with sixteen articles

1. Lights
2. Incense
3. Flowers
4. Cloth
5. Sacred Thread
6. Rudrākṣa
7. Sindūr
8. Kumkum
9. Sandal Paste
10. Mālā
11. Food offering
12. Water
13. Umbrella
14. Fly whisk
15. Fan
16. Mirror

Worship can be performed with more than sixteen articles

Any more than sixteen articles is known as Rājopacāra, an offering of a King.

There are different baths, scents, jewels, ornaments, the list is limited only by imagination.

Śiva has five faces

1. Sadyojāta
the Birth of Truth as Pure Existence
2. Vāmadeva
Beautiful God Who Is Beloved
3. Aghora
He Who Is Free From Fear
4. Tat Puruṣa
That Universal Consciousness
5. Īśāna
Seer of All

Hṛdayādi nyāsaḥ is also called ṣadaṅga nyāsaḥ because it touches six points on the body

1. Touch heart
2. Top of head
3. Back of head
4. Cross both arms
5. Touch three eyes
6. Roll hand over hand forwards
and backwards and clap hands

Seven rivers run through the land where the Light of Wisdom shines

1. Gaṅgā
2. Jamunā
3. Godāvarī
4. Sarasvatī
5. Narmadā
6. Sindhu
7. Kāverī

The Divine Fire has seven tongues

1. Kālī	Black
2. Karālī	Increasing, formidable
3. Mano-javā	Swift as thought
4. Su-Lohitā	Excellent shine
5. Sudhūmra-Varnā	Purple
6. Ugrā or Sphulingīnī	Fearful
7. Pradīptā	Giving light

There are eight forms of siddhi, attainment of spiritual powers

1. Animā
Being small
2. Laghimā
Being light
3. Mahimā
Being great
4. Prāpti
Fulfilling desire
5. Prākāmya
Sufficiency
6. Isitva
Rulership
7. Vaśitva
Control
8. Sarvajñātva
Omniscience

There are eight forms of Śakti or Energy

1. Brāhmī
Creative Energy
2. Nārāyaṇī
Exposer of Consciousness
3. Māheśvarī
Energy of the Seer of All
4. Cāmuṇḍā
Slayer of Passion and Meanness
5. Kaumārī
The Ever Pure One
6. Aparājitā
The Unconquerable
7. Vārāhī
The Boar of Sacrifice
8. Nārasiṃhī
The Man-Lion of Courage

There are nine forms of Durgā

1. Śailaputrī
Goddess of Inspiration
2. Brahmacāriṇī
Goddess of Sacred Study
3. Candraghaṇṭā
Goddess of the Delight of Practice
4. Kūṣmāṇḍā
Goddess of Purifying Austerity
5. Skandamātā
Goddess who Nurtures Divinity
6. Kātyāyanī
Goddess Who is Ever Pure
7. Kālarātrī
Goddess of the Dark Night of
Overcoming Egotism
8. Mahāgaurī
Goddess of the Great Radiant Light
9. Siddhidātrī
Goddess who Grants Perfection

There are nine planets, Nava Graha

1. Sūrya
Sun, Light of Wisdom, Dispeller of Ignorance
2. Soma
Moon, emblem of devotion
3. Maṅgala
Mars, Bearer of Welfare
4. Buddha
Mercury, the emblem of Intelligence
5. Bṛhāspati
Jupiter, Guru of the Gods
6. Śukra
Venus, the emblem of love and attachment
7. Śanaiścara
Saturn, the emblem of control
8. Rāhu
North Node, who commands direction
9. Ketu
South Node, who presents obstacles

There are ten Mahāvidyās

1. Kālī
2. Bagalā
3. Cinnamastā
4. Bhuvaneśvarī
5. Mātaṅgī
6. Śorasī
7. Dhūmāvatī
8. Tripurasundarī
9. Tārā
10. Bhairavī

1. Kālī takes away the darkness and is beyond time
2. Bagalā stops all motion at the appropriate time
3. Cinnamastā demonstrates the courage to make sacrifice
4. Bhuvaneśvarī is the Supreme of manifested existence
5. Mātaṅgī is the measurement of all the limbs of creation
6. Śorasī unites the sixteen syllables of Śiva and Śakti
7. Dhūmāvatī demonstrates renunciation and removes all frustration
8. Tripurasundarī is the beauty of all the threes
9. Tārā is the illuminator of all attitudes
10. Bhairavī is free from any kind of fear

There are ten Protectors of the ten Directions

1. Indra	East
2. Agni	South-East
3. Yama	South
4. Nairrita	South-West
5. Varuṇa	West
6. Vāyu	North-West
7. Kuvera (Soma)	North
8. Īśāna	North-East
9. Brahmā	Above
10. Viṣṇu (Ananta)	Below

Viṣṇu has ten Āvatāras, special incarnations which manifest

1. Matsyā
2. Kūrmma
3. Vārāha
4. Nṛsiṃha
5. Vāmana
6. Paraśurāma
7. Rāma
8. Kṛṣṇa
9. Buddha
10. Kalki

There are eleven forms of Rudra

1. Kedārnāth
2. Bhīmāśaṅkara
3. Baijanāth
4. Nāgeśvara
5. Rāmeśvara
6. Oṃkāreśvara
7. Mamaleśvara
8. Mahākāla
9. Mallikārjuna
10. Tryaṃbaka
11. Somanāth

There are twelve Jyotir Lingams

1. Somanātham
2. Mallikārjunam
3. Mahākālam
4. Oṃkāreśvaram
5. Kedāranātham
6. Bhīmaśaṅkaram
7. Viśveśvaram
8. Tryambakam
9. Baijanātham
10. Nāgeśvaram
11. Rāmeśvaram
12. Ghuśmeśvaram

There are twelve Ādityas, original Vedic Gods, the sons of Aditi

1. Indra
2. Agnī
3. Mitrā
4. Varuṇa
5. Pūṣa
6. Aryaman
7. Sūrya
8. Soma
9. Bhaga
10. Vasū
11. Savitar
12. Aśvin

There are 51 Śakti Pithas

There are 57 deities of the Sarva Badra Maṅdala

There are 64 Yoginis

There are 108 Siddha Pithas

There are a thousand names for each deity

There are a thousand petals in the lotus of the crown cakra

And then we reach to Uttara Mīmāṃsā

And that means Vedānta in which all is

One

The famous proclamation of Vedānta is

Brahmā satyā jagat mityā

The Supreme Divinity is true
and the world is not.

Consciousness is always the same and therefore it is true and abiding. The world is always changing and therefore it is false.

There are three forms of Māyā

Māyā of Vedānta
Māyā of Tantra
Māyā of Śāṅkhyā

Māyā of Śāṅkhyā is defined as the illusion which obscures the reality

Māyā of Tantra is the embodiment of the Divine Mother

Māyā of Vedānta is the measurement of consciousness

The Kādi mantra of Śrī Vidyā defines the three forms of Māyā

How God sees Herself

How God sees the world and
the world sees God

How the world sees the world

Māyā as illusion
Māyā as the universal body of Nature
Māyā as the One Consciousness in
harmony with its own self

The mantra says:
ka e ī la hrīṃ
ha sa ka ha la hrīṃ
sa ka la hrīṃ

This understanding is the behavior of excellence, Kulācaraṇa.

As we move from sitting in one-pointed meditation in samādhi to interacting with the world, the bhāva remains the same. We become the embodiment of the ideal as described in Iśopaniṣāda:

Those who worship by means of the body overcome death, and those who worship by means of the spirit achieve immortality.

We realize that the changes of Nature are constant

Oṃ aiṃ hrīṃ klīṃ
cāmuṇḍāyai vicce

All of the threes are in continual movement in the perception of Consciousness

And that Consciousness am I

Oṃ namaḥ Śivāya

I bow to the Consciousness
of Infinite Goodness

The face of the real is hidden by illusions of the mind, formed by the thoughts of procurement and attainment. But the spirit is in the Light rather than its rays, and that Spirit am I.

Oṃ - the Light - the Supreme Divinity

For more information or if you have questions, please contact us:

www.shreemaa.org

Books by Shree Maa and Swami Satyananda Saraswati

Annapūrṇa Thousand Names
Before Becoming This
Bhagavad Gītā
Chaṇḍi Pāṭh
Chaṇḍi Pāṭh - Study of Chapter One
Chaṇḍi Pāṭh - Study of Chapter Two
Cosmic Pūjā
Cosmic Pūjā Bengali
Devī Gītā
Devī Mandir Songbook
Durgā Pūjā Beginner
Ganeśa Pūjā
Gāyatrī Sahasra Nāma
Guru Gītā
Hanumān Pūjā
Kālī Pūjā
Lakṣmī Sahasra Nāma
Lalitā Triśati
Pronunciation and the Chaṇḍi Sampuṭs
Rudrāṣṭādhyāyī
Sahib Sadhu
Saraswati Pūjā for Children
Shree Maa's Favorite Recipes
Shree Maa - The Guru & the Goddess
Shree Maa, The Life of a Saint
Śiva Pūjā Beginner
Śiva Pūjā and Advanced Fire Ceremony
Sundara Kāṇḍa
Swāmī Purāṇa
Tattva Jñāna
Thousand Names of Gāyatrī
Thousand Names of Viṣṇu and
Satya Nārāyaṇa Vrata Kathā

CPSIA information can be obtained
at www.ICGtesting.com
Printed in the USA
JSHW041500060723
44091JS00013B/1